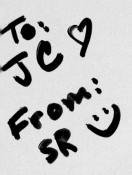

To:
JC ♥
From:
SR ☺

VOTES
→ FOR ←
WOMEN!

Images from the

SUFFRAGE
MOVEMENT

MW00533457

Pomegranate
PORTLAND, OREGON

LIBRARY
LIBRARY OF CONGRESS

Pomegranate Communications, Inc.
19018 NE Portal Way, Portland, OR 97230
800-227-1428   www.pomegranate.com

Pomegranate Europe
Number 3 Siskin Drive, Middlemarch Business Park
Coventry, CV3 4FJ, UK
+44 (0)24 7621 4461   sales@pomegranate.com

Pomegranate publishes books of postcards on a wide range of subjects.
Please contact the publisher for more information.

Front cover: Adapted from cover for "Votes for Women International Suffragists' Song,"
artist unknown, written and published by Ed Markel, 1916

Back cover: Mary Winsor (1869–1956) protested the treatment of imprisoned suffragists,
who endured solitary confinement and force-feeding in 1917. Winsor was arrested twice herself.

ISBN 978-0-7649-8661-1
Item No. AA1052

Cover designed by Stephanie Odeh

Printed in Korea

28 27 26 25 24 23 22 21 20 19   10 9 8 7 6 5 4 3 2 1

To facilitate detachment of the postcards from this book, fold each card along its perforation line before tearing.

AMERICAN WOMEN fought for more than seven decades to earn the right to vote. During that time, they organized, lectured, petitioned, lobbied, paraded, picketed, and went to jail for daring to support suffrage. The movement questioned the country's commitment to democracy, highlighted persistent racial and class tensions, and challenged domestic relationships. It shaped the individuals involved in the struggle, at times demanding enormous personal sacrifice.

In the early days of the republic, women had few rights. Most married women could not own property, a common requirement for voting; enslaved women, considered property themselves, essentially had no legal rights. Inspired by the growing abolition movement, women began advocating for their own rights by the mid-nineteenth century. The 1848 Seneca Falls Convention in New York was the first of many gatherings dedicated to advancing women's equality. Following the upheaval of the Civil War, the expansion of civil rights for African Americans during Reconstruction ignited a renewed effort for universal suffrage, though disagreements over strategy divided the movement.

In the twentieth century, the next generation of suffrage leaders introduced new tactics. Adopting strategies used by the British suffrage movement, activists held open-air meetings and parades. Beginning in 1917, and throughout World War I, the National

Woman's Party staged a sustained daily protest at the White House, decrying the hypocrisy of America's defense of democracy abroad while women were denied the vote at home. Some picketers were arrested and imprisoned, bringing visibility to the movement and forcing the suffrage question onto the front pages of newspapers and magazines. The combination of civil disobedience and political lobbying eventually produced results, leading to the ratification of the Nineteenth Amendment in 1920. Few of the women who began the suffrage campaign before the Civil War lived to witness its victory.

The images in this postcard book are drawn from the collections of the Library of Congress, which houses the records of the National American Woman Suffrage Association and the National Woman's Party, as well as papers of prominent suffragists, including Susan B. Anthony, Elizabeth Cady Stanton, Carrie Chapman Catt, and Mary Church Terrell. The Library's unparalleled archive of photographs, periodicals, broadsides, and ephemera illustrates how the suffrage debate permeated popular culture and highlights the courage and sacrifice that sustained the movement.

VOTES FOR WOMEN!

This illustration for *Puck* (March 14, 1914) by Gordon Grant (1875–1962) depicts youthful foot soldiers of the suffrage movement advocating for voting rights. The original caption reads, "Giddap! Friendly Farmer.—Can't I give ye a lift, girls? Suffragette 'General.'—You can, sir, by voting for the Cause!"

www.pomegranate.com

Pomegranate

VOTES FOR WOMEN!

As the first president of the National Association of Colored Women, educator and activist Mary Church Terrell (1863–1954) worked tirelessly to advance the rights of African Americans and to win women the right to vote.

www.pomegranate.com

Pomegranate

VOTES FOR WOMEN!

As president of the National American Woman Suffrage Association, Carrie Chapman Catt (1859–1947) created both state and federal lobbying strategies and ensured state legislatures would ratify the Nineteenth Amendment.

National Photo Company, 1909–1932
Prints and Photographs Division, Library of Congress

www.pomegranate.com

Pomegranate

VOTES FOR WOMEN!

Martha Wentworth Suffern (1859–1957) was vice chair of
the Woman Suffrage Party of New York, an organization
founded by Carrie Chapman Catt as a political machine to
unite the campaign for the vote in New York state.

Bain News Service, 1914
Prints and Photographs Division, Library of Congress

www.pomegranate.com

Pomegranate

VOTES FOR WOMEN!

Upon their marriage, activist Lucy Stone (1818–1893) and Henry Blackwell published a statement protesting the unequal legal protections offered to married men and women. Stone kept her maiden name, a radical choice during that time.

www.pomegranate.com

Pomegranate

Life

Price 15 Cents

October 28, 1920

Vol. 76. Copyright, 1920. Life Publishing Company. No. 1982

VOTES FOR WOMEN!

Published on the eve of the first presidential election in which all women had the right to vote, this cover for *Life* (October 28, 1920) by Charles Dana Gibson (1867–1944), titled *Congratulations*, shows the figure of Columbia, representing the United States, acknowledging a young woman with ballot in hand.

Pomegranate

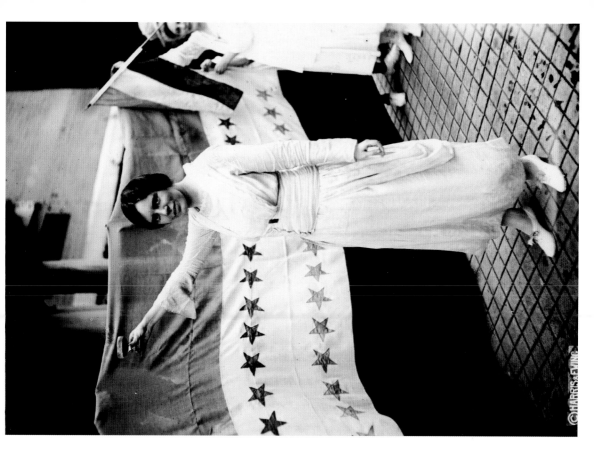

VOTES FOR WOMEN!

Trained on the front lines of Britain's suffrage movement,
Alice Paul (1885–1977) cofounded the National Woman's Party,
which mounted confrontational protests and picketed the
White House to demand voting rights for women in America.
Shown here in 1920, Paul celebrates the ratification of the
Nineteenth Amendment.

Harris and Ewing
Prints and Photographs Division, Library of Congress

www.pomegranate.com

Pomegranate

VOTES FOR WOMEN!

Duncan Grant (1885–1978) was a joint winner in the British Artists' Suffrage League poster competition with this 1909 work, *Handicapped!*, which illustrates the ease with which men sail with the vote, while women struggle to row choppy waters without it.

Prints and Photographs Division, Library of Congress

www.pomegranate.com

Pomegranate

VOTES FOR WOMEN!

Suffragists carried tricolor banners up the steps of the
US Capitol in 1917, one of many dramatic demonstrations
designed to gain supporters for women's voting rights.

Harris and Ewing
Prints and Photographs Division, Library of Congress

www.pomegranate.com

Pomegranate

I Sell the Shadow to Support the Substance.

SOJOURNER TRUTH.

VOTES FOR WOMEN!

Born into slavery, Sojourner Truth (c. 1797–1883) was a prominent abolitionist and suffragist. She sold *cartes de visite* like this one from 1864 to earn money, hence the message, "I sell the shadow to support the substance."

Prints and Photographs Division, Library of Congress

VOTES FOR WOMEN!

The allegorical figure of Justice demands voting rights for both wealthy and working women, as pictured in the foreground of this 1909 poster by the Artists' Suffrage League, a group founded to provide visual materials for the women's suffrage movement in Britain.

Prints and Photographs Division, Library of Congress

www.pomegranate.com

Pomegranate

VOTES FOR WOMEN!

Posted outside the White House in 1917, Suzanne Morin Swing (1882–1982) protested the hypocrisy of the United States' claim to defend democracy in World War I, when American women did not have the right to vote.

Harris and Ewing
Prints and Photographs Division, Library of Congress

VOTES FOR WOMEN!

When the United States entered World War I in 1917, some suffragists used the war to intensify their rhetoric. This suffragist's banner reads, "Mr. President: it is unjust to deny women a voice in their government when the government is conscripting their sons."

Harris and Ewing
Prints and Photographs Division, Library of Congress

www.pomegranate.com

Pomegranate

VOTES FOR WOMEN!

Benjamin M. Dale (1889–1951) created the official program for
the Woman Suffrage Procession, a demonstration that brought
thousands to Washington, DC, on March 3, 1913, the day before
President Woodrow Wilson's first inauguration.

Prints and Photographs Division, Library of Congress

www.pomegranate.com

Pomegranate

VOTES FOR WOMEN!

Mary Winsor (1869–1956) protested the treatment of
imprisoned suffragists, who endured solitary confinement
and force-feeding in 1917. Winsor was arrested twice herself.

Harris and Ewing
Prints and Photographs Division, Library of Congress

www.pomegranate.com

Pomegranate

Life

PRICE 10 CENTS

Vol. 66, No. 1705, July 1, 1915

Copyright, 1915, Life Publishing Company

IN CONGRESS, July 1, 1776.

The unanimous Declaration of the thirteen united States of America.

We hold these truths to be self-evident that all men *and women* are created equal

VOTES FOR WOMEN!

The women's suffrage movement sought legitimacy by aligning itself with the ideals of the American Revolution. On this cover for *Life* (July 1, 1915), *1776—Retouching an Old Masterpiece—1915*, by Paul Stahr (1883–1953), a young suffragist amends the Declaration of Independence while an unidentified founding father looks on.

General Collections, Library of Congress

www.pomegranate.com

Pomegranate

VOTES FOR WOMEN!

Renowned British suffragist Emmeline Pankhurst (1858–1928)
addressed a crowd on Wall Street in New York City during an
American lecture tour in 1911.

Bain News Service
Prints and Photographs Division, Library of Congress

VOTES FOR WOMEN!

By 1915, women had full voting rights in eleven states clustered in the West. Henry Mayer (1868–1954) depicted women clamoring for their rights as progress moved eastward in this illustration, *The Awakening*, for *Puck* (February 20, 1915).

Prints and Photographs Division, Library of Congress

www.pomegranate.com

Pomegranate

VOTES FOR WOMEN!

In 1917, state, professional, or other affiliated groups organized daily pickets of the White House. Wage-earning women picketed on February 18, 1917.

Harris and Ewing
Prints and Photographs Division, Library of Congress

www.pomegranate.com

Pomegranate

VOTES FOR WOMEN!

Suffragists invited New York City mayor William Jay Gaynor to join them in a hay-wagon ride through the streets of Manhattan while en route to their tent at the Empire City Park Fair in Yonkers in 1913. He declined.

Bain News Service
Prints and Photographs Division, Library of Congress

www.pomegranate.com

Pomegranate

VOTES FOR WOMEN!

For five decades, Susan B. Anthony (1820–1906) and
Elizabeth Cady Stanton (1815–1902) led the campaign for
women's voting rights. Of Anthony's organizing prowess
and her own skillful theorizing, Stanton said, "I forged the
thunderbolts and she fired them."

Edmonston, c. 1891
Manuscript Division, Library of Congress

www.pomegranate.com

Pomegranate

VOTES FOR WOMEN!

Alison Turnbull Hopkins (1880–1951), New Jersey state chair
of the National Woman's Party, picketed the White House on
New Jersey Day, January 30, 1917.

Manuscript Division, Library of Congress

www.pomegranate.com

Pomegranate

VOTES FOR WOMEN!

In January 1917, the National Woman's Party began daily protests at the White House. These picketers from New York sought President Woodrow Wilson's support for a constitutional amendment granting women the right to vote.

Manuscript Division, Library of Congress

www.pomegranate.com

Pomegranate

VOTES FOR WOMEN

INTERNATIONAL SUFFRAGISTS' SONG

BY ED. MARKEL

25¢

Ed. Markel, Publisher, Des Moines, Ia.
911 W. 18TH STREET

VOTES FOR WOMEN!

Suffrage imagery decorated numerous sheet music covers,
whether or not the songs related to voting rights. An
unknown artist created this cover for "Votes for Women
International Suffragists' Song," written and published by
Ed Markel in 1916.

Music Division, Library of Congress

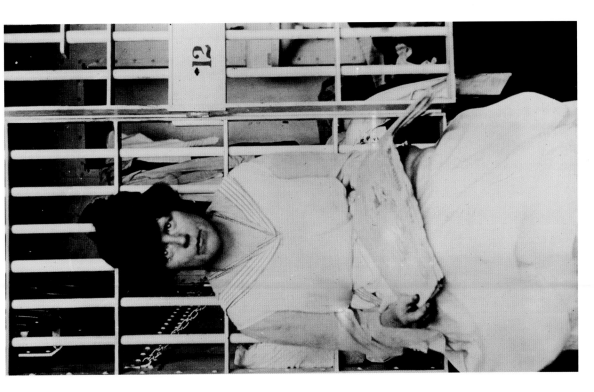

VOTES FOR WOMEN!

National Woman's Party leader Lucy Burns (1879–1966),
shown here at what's likely Occoquan Workhouse in
1917, spent more time in prison than any other suffragist
in America, after multiple arrests for leading picket
demonstrations.

Harris and Ewing
Manuscript Division, Library of Congress

www.pomegranate.com

Pomegranate

VOTES FOR WOMEN!

Disconcerted by the unequal treatment women faced in the abolition movement, Quaker minister Lucretia Mott (1793–1880) joined with Elizabeth Cady Stanton to plan the first women's rights convention, in Seneca Falls, New York, in 1848.

F. Gutekunst, c. 1875
Manuscript Division, Library of Congress

www.pomegranate.com

Pomegranate

VOTES FOR WOMEN!

Emulating the style of an ancient Greek vase, *We Want Our Rights* by Rea Irvin (1881–1972) pokes fun at suffragists with his depiction of Susan B. Anthony armed with an umbrella, published as a cover for *Life* (February 20, 1913).

Prints and Photographs Division, Library of Congress

VOTES FOR WOMEN!

National Woman's Party members picketed President
Woodrow Wilson's speech in Chicago in 1916, urging his
support for women's suffrage. Both African American
and white women participated in the demonstration.

Manuscript Division, Library of Congress

www.pomegranate.com

Pomegranate

VOTES FOR WOMEN!

Elizabeth Smith Miller (1822–1911) was a suffragist and
dress-reform advocate. She is pictured here in a costume of
her own design in 1851. Popularized in Amelia Bloomer's
newspaper, *The Lily*, the loose trousers became known as
bloomers.

Manuscript Division, Library of Congress

VOTES FOR WOMEN!

The August 19, 1920, cover for *Life* by Rea Irvin (1881–1972) was published just after the ratification of the Nineteenth Amendment and bore the caption "What next?"

General Collections, Library of Congress